I0532661

Who's Walking With Me

Who's Walking With Me

ISBN: 979-8-9889305-1-8 (Paperback Edition)
ISBN: 979-8-9889305-2-5 (eBook Edition)

Printed in the United States of America

Publication Date January, 2024

For information about this title or to order books and/or electronic media, contact the publisher:

Sula Too Publishing
sulatoollc@gmail.com
www.sulatoo.com/publishing
813-200-8878

Who's Walking With Me

LaWanda "Queen" Armstrong

Sula Too Publishing

Dedication

*I would like to dedicate this book
to my family, friends, and
followers on Facebook.*

*To the people in my community
who supported me and
" Who's Walking With Me"*

*Enjoy and keep on walking with me!
I never knew all of this
would become a book,
but it's all part of God's plan,
not mine.*

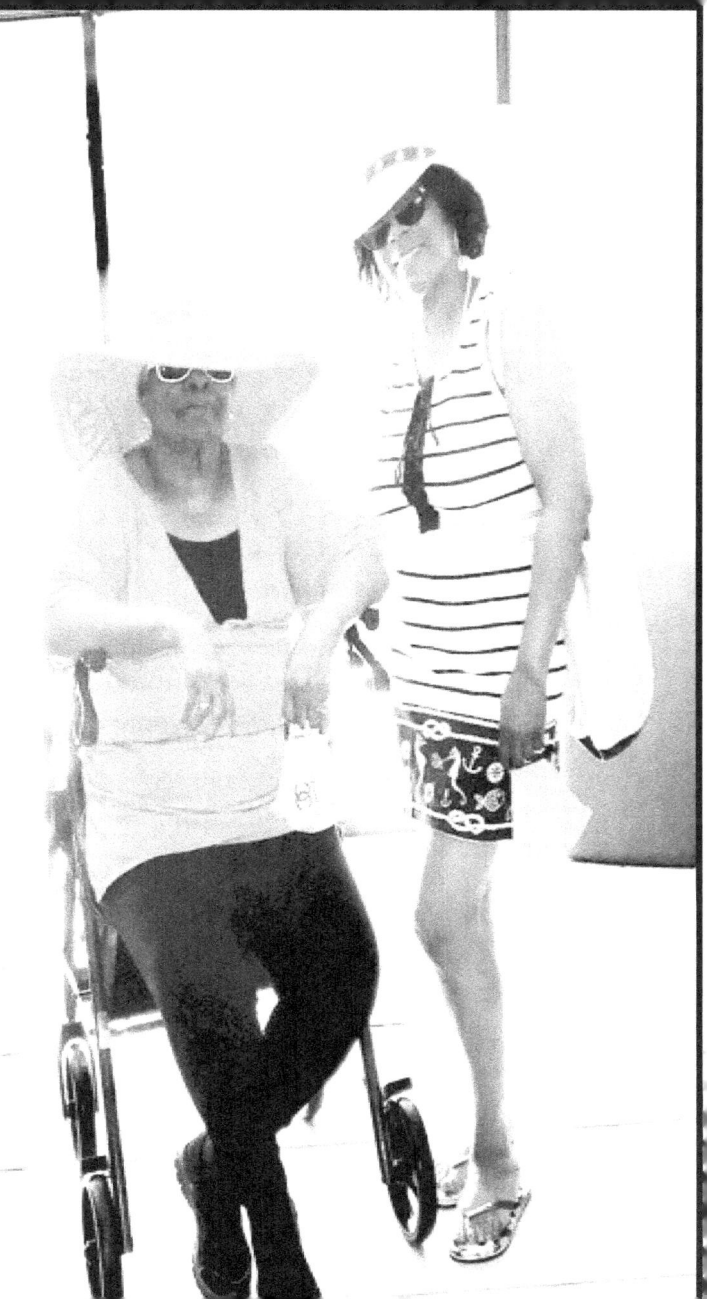

Day 1

Good morning family and friends!

*Today, I am starting my day with God.
He is the way and the light of my life.*

*He brings me out of the darkness.
He gives me peace, joy, and comfort.
Whenever I have a problem, I talk to him.*

*I do not need a phone.
I just open up and start talking.
To add to that
I'm walking and talking to God now.*

*I tell him all about me; my visions, my
dreams, my goals; and my plans.*

*When I visualize my life,
I see myself working for the Lord
by helping others.*

*I plan to follow through
on the path the Lord has for me.
He already knows everything about me.*

*So, I pray He takes control. Lord, whatever
your plan is for me, let your will be done
and don't let me make the same mistakes
over and over again.*

Day 2

Who's walking with me?

*The first time I started walking,
I was so full. Full of hurt.*

*I didn't know what to do because my feelings and emotions were in the way.
I could not see past them.*

So, I hurt inside, and loneliness set in.

*I would often wonder
about my past relationship and
how I could have made it different.*

*The more I walked
the clearer things became to me.*

*"Everything comes together for the good
of the Lord."*

*On this new journey,
I started to realize that I was not alone.*

*I learned that God was with me
the entire time I had been walking.*

Day 3

When I look in the mirror,
I see myself.
I look beyond my brown skin and
see this beautiful woman who loves God.

I desire to give nothing more
than my best in all I do.

But I know I am a long way
from being perfect.

I taught my children
what I have learned--to love and give love,
to be strong in life,
and to do what they love.

I'm always telling them
about eating right, exercising,
and never giving up.

The most important thing
I have taught them is how to look to God
who is our help in everything we do in life.

Moreover, I've taught them that
learning from our mistakes does not
make us weak but makes us stronger.
It is only when you look back that
you can be strong, overcome your failures,
and become successful.

Day 4

Who's walking with me?

*I'm still walking by faith
and not by sight.*

*Starting over is not easy.
But start walking because,
with every step you take,
you get better and stronger.*

*Consider the grass that grows and
when it gets cut,
it grows back thicker and stronger.*

*Sometimes that is how life can be.
It gets cut. It can be your job, your relationship, or your finances.*

Things can get cut.

*We have to live like the grass
when we get cut.
We must know we will grow again
until it will not grow anymore.*

Living things always grow.

Day 5

Who's walking with me?

I am so grateful to be alive
To be able to get up and rise
like the sun and
shine in someone's life.

For filling their mind with inspiration
and giving them hope to keep going.

We never know
which way the wind may blow.

So, keep your head up and
keep walking towards your goal
or you can't go on anymore.

Remember, we only get one life to live.
Decide to live it to the fullest.

Day 6

Who's walking with me?
I want to fill my life with every
great thought I can think of.

Like eating ice cream
on a cloudy day--fulfilling my
dreams in every possible way.

Playing my guitar and keyboard
to the sound of the beat
I hear on the inside in my mind.
Dreaming out loud under a cloud.

Or not hearing other people's thoughts
on their wants.
Because at the end of the day,
it's the way you see life.

The way you may see things
is not the way others may see them.

It's your dream. Go for it!
And walk it out
no matter how long it might take.
Keep walking until you get there.

Day 7

Who's walking with me?
I gained weight and was
having a hard time losing it.

No matter which diet plan I used
or how much walking I did,
I struggled to lose weight.
Until I got sick and found out
I had an infection in my stomach.

With that discovery,
the weight started dropping off.
I never gave up I focused on,
eating and living.

Don't give up on yourself.

Day 8

Be encouraged in everything you do.

*When it looks like
it is not going to happen,
don't quit.*

*Keep going because
life can be complicated and
you will become frustrated
but wait on God.*

*And he will bring you through
the storm of life because
it does not always last.*

*I was walking while I was sick and
did not know if I would get better.*

*I prayed to God to help me
when I could not eat.*

*I would have to blend my food,
sip liquids slowly, walking and encourage
others not to give up on themselves.It got
so bad I had to go to the hospital.*

*The Lord was helping me to get better.
I still watch what I eat, walk every day,
and with the help of the Lord,
that spirit lives in me.*

Day 9

Who's Walking With Me?
At the end of the day it is about me.
To live and to die,
I cry and try to do my best.

Some days are better than others.
But do I quit? No, I have to keep going
because nobody can do it for me.

Whatever it is or whatever you want,
you have to make it happen.
Get to know your strengths
mentally and physically.
Acknowledge how much you
can and   cannot take.

I walk 30 minutes five days a week.
A co-worker saw me walking and asked
"How long do you walk?"
I told her 30 minutes, she suggested
that I walk an hour. I told her,
"No, 30 minutes is good enough for me.

Never let somebody change your routine,
they may offer suggestions but
that does not mean you have to do it.
Keep on walking if you can and
eventually you will see the
change in yourself mentally and physically.

Day 10

Good morning my family and friends!

*Today I come to bring you a shining light
to lift you in the spirit. Because without it
you are dead and cannot move.*

*If you can get up then
put up an effort to do better for yourself.*

Tell yourself what it is you need to do.

*For instance, eat right because
it is going to help you feel better.*

*Sleep right because
it is going to help you to perform better.*

*Exercise because
it is going to help keep you moving right.*

*And let's not forget to pray because
we need God in our lives. Especially since
He made us with love in mind
to enjoy the world we live in.*

Day 11

In the beginning,
God created everything and
it was good including
the air we breathe.

He created the sun so that
we can see, stay warm, and to keep our
bones strong with vitamin D.

God created water for us to drink,
so our bodies can function and
water the plants we enjoy as
the fruits of the land.

He taught us through Adam and Eve
what happens when we eat
from the tree of bad fruit.

He gave us a brain to know good from bad.
We all should learn through life
for it will teach us the difference.

Look up when you are feeling down.
There is something greater than all of us
that can help us to be healthy and fit.

Day 12

Who's walking with me?
My family.

One of the things I taught my children
is to take care of their bodies
and to eat right.

They watch me walk and work out
and are inspired to work out too.
I am so proud of them!

Even if they fall,
they know how to get back up.

I believe teaching starts from your home.
Whatever you teach in the home will come
out of it through your children.

I even taught them to eat right
so they know when they get off track
and that they can find their way back.

Eat right, stay tight, work out.

That's what it is all about
in this life we live today.

Day 13

Who's walking with me?
I am.
I'm learning more and more about myself.
This morning I got up
and made my mom and me a smoothie.
I went out for my walk and enjoyed myself.
The weather was good, not too hot,
and not too cold. It was just right.

While I was walking,
I began listening to a YouTube video
on faith and how not to let
worry take control of you.

I'm walking forward in life. Believing that
God is with me in everything I do.
Learning that I have to be bold in my faith
because God will help me build courage.
I just have to seek and I will find.

The guide is in the book of Deuteronomy
31:6, "Be strong and of good courage.
Do not fear, nor be afraid of them for the
Lord your God.
He is the one who goes with you.
He will not leave nor forsake you."
So let us trust in him
to get us through this life we live.

Day 14

I am walking
and enjoying myself at the same time.

I'm enjoying others who walk with me and
the ones who say they are walking.

I like to hear them say
they are inspired by my words.

When I see others walking,
it inspires me to take another step.

Step by step we will make this journey to
better ourselves.

On my daily walk,
I see people walking on the track,
in the park, and the graveyard.

It just lets me know walking is good
everywhere you go.

Day 15

Good morning, world!

It is so good to see you all walking with me.

**I love to hear the ones who say they are
about to get started.**

**It does not matter
what state they are in;
they are still
walking with me,
Lady Queen.**

**It's time to stay in shape,
no time to waste.
This way we can fight off a lot of things
like obesity by burning calories and
keeping our weight under control.**

Day 16

*Your mind is a terrible thing
to waste because
without it you are no good
to yourself or others.*

*You see God gave you the gift to live
and to do good with your life.*

*Your mind is a terrible thing to waste.
Your mind is a tool to use in building
and doing great things.*

*It also helps us to
even use our failures
to become successful.*

It helps us know right from wrong.

*And to be aware of
what is going on in the world today.*

*We need to know what side
we need to be on
in order to utilize our intelligence.*

Day 17

I love the beach because it relaxes me.
Come take a walk with me
and you will see.

The ocean sets me free.

Don't talk, just listen.

Do not even talk on the phone.

You will miss the peace and calmness that
gives you a break from your wandering
mind from having to think all the time.

The ocean water brushes on your feet.
The warm water relaxes your body
while you toss, turn,
and bounce up and down in the waves.

Don't speak for a little while.
Let's just be quiet and
enjoy the moment.

Day 18

I'm not afraid of you,
because you are beautiful.

I'm not afraid of change.
It is time to see new things and grow.

It's time to move forward and
see what life has in store for you.
So, keep walking and do not look back.

When I look at you in the mirror,
I see myself and there is
no way I can leave you behind.

Because we are one.
I just need to realize that
and get out of my own way.
To look deep inside to pull me up.

It's time to walk it out and
see what life has for me.
And to change for the better.
Becoming stronger in my growth
by accepting myself for myself
and letting it be what it is regardless of
what I have to go through.

Day 19

Wake up!

It has been weeks and
I'm still walking.
I have not looked back.
I am still climbing
the mountain in my mind.

It is really high,
and I am not even halfway up but
I'm not on the bottom.
I am a fighter and
I have got a long way to go yet,

I'm pushing my way through.

I will never know
what tomorrow may bring
for today I'm still walking.

Day 20

I am my best friend because
I know everything about me.

When things go wrong,
I know how to fix them.

I know what makes me happy and
I know what makes me sad.

I know how to turn things around
when things seem upside down
and I frown.

I know how to stop my tears and
get rid of my fears.
I just talk to God and
everything will be alright.

I know all my secrets
better than anyone else and
I plan to make some changes.

Day 21

I thank God for
waking me up this morning
in my right mind.
Because someone else did not.

Some people do not remember yesterday.
I see people who do not know
who their children are or
what kind of food they are eating.
Some may not even recall their own name.

Let's cherish the life we have.

Thank God for the people
that are still in your life.
And for what you have in life.

Stop worrying about
what other people have.
Because you do not know
what it took for them to get there.
Or what it's going to take
to keep them there.

Life is like a museum.
You look and you keep walking.

Day 22

I am so glad you found me.

I was lost and
my life was turned inside out.

Without a doubt,
I knew I had to fight.
To break through many chains
to get my life on track and
I am still walking it out.

The demon is chasing me day and night.
Fighting me on the job to wear me out.

Without a doubt,
I put down my anchor and
began to walk and talk with
God who always helps me out.

Day 23

The way to get ahead is getting started.
You have got to take the steps to go far.

You have got to think about it, then,
write it down on paper.
And start pushing it where it should go.

You cannot be afraid to be you. Because
God is out in front of you and Jesus is
walking right beside you.

Step out on faith.
And do not look back,
just keep walking and trust in Him.

What is it that you want to do?
If you mess up, just know that eventually,
you will get it right.

For God knows what you need. So be
ready! Things are going to come and get
you off track but it is just a test.

Stay focused!

Day 24

To walk your way to good

health, you need a sound mind. Do not let life pass you by.

Always have some goals in mind.

If you are in poverty, come up with a plan to move up in the world.

You have to lift yourself by your bootstraps and not wait for someone else to have your back.

It is always feels better when you look back and can say,

"I did it for myself."

Day 25

Prayer works and I know
because I do it all the time.
When I fall short,
I ask the creator
to lift me out of my darkness,
my sadness, my suffering,
and my loneliness.

And he helps me
by removing it through my feelings
and lifting me with his love.

Then joy and laughter come
by reminding me
that these things will come but will not
always last.

Trust in the Lord and
he will never let you down;
he will always lift you out of your trials
and make you strong.

Even when you feel alone,
God will strengthen you and
your life will prosper.

Day 26

*Do not ever give up when life
throws you a curveball.*

Keep on trying until you hit a home run.

*Sometimes life will put a stumbling block
in your way to make you fall.
But get back up,
dust yourself off and keep on trying.*

*Hold on to God.
God has a plan for you.*

*Nothing is lost unless you give up.
Rise and push through.
Eventually,
you will push your way through.*

*Love yourself.
That way you will not hurt so bad
when your heart feels broken.*

*You will be able to
put the pieces back together
that were there
when you first came into the world.*

Day 27

Worry will not get you to where

you need to go. Make the decision or choice to take your problem to God. God will bear the burden of your problem and the stress will be less.

Whatever you are going through, work it out instead of allowing what you know to control and take over. Slow down, listen to your heart, and let it guide you when your mind is telling you what to do.

Slow down when it comes to love and listen to your heart. It will never fail you.

Let God's will be done and ask him to help you when you are not sure. Open up, listen, and wait for Him to respond.

Day 28

Let your gift grow.

When I think of a gift,
it all starts with a vision in my head.

A shock to the body parts
so that my mind and body move as one
with my thoughts.

Whatever you are trying to accomplish,
you are going to give 100 percent because
it is moving in tune.

You cannot fail.

Failure is not an option because
I am on top of my game.

If I start lacking mentally,
my physical aspect will
kick in and takeover

Day 29

My workout is important.

If I miss a day,
I feel like I have forgotten about myself.

I must spend time with myself and
have talks with God.

My live video
encouraged others to get involved and
take care of themselves first.

Because we can get caught up
in other people's situations,
we can truly lose our balance
if we don't spend time with ourselves.

Remember to love yourself first.
You will know your strength and
get to know yourself better.

Day 30

Walking has changed my life.

When I do not walk,
I lose my sight
I pray and ask God
to get me right.
It is a fight
trying to live
a bright
life.

When I see something
that will complete me,
I search my heart and realize
it is just something
I want and not what I need.

So, I keep walking.
God, please help me when the time is right.

And keep my focus on you because
you know exactly what I need.

Day 31

Walking has changed my life.

When I do not walk,
I get uptight and keep pushing
to get it right.

Sometimes I lose my sight but it is okay.
I am not perfect.

I just tell myself it is time to
get back on track
and start over.

Day 32

A thousand-mile journey begins with one step.

Once you begin and take the first step of the thousand-mile journey, no one knows when it will end but God.

Day 33

Sometimes in life,
you have to take two steps backward
to take two steps forward in life because
failure is a great achievement.

It teaches you not
to do that same thing again.

By chance, you do it again,
pick yourself up and start all over
until you get it right.

Day 34

*Every step I have taken in life
was a learning experience because
you are going to go through ups and downs
in life.*

*We have to learn how to deal with it and
balance it out.*

*There is no one way in life
so do not stop just keep walking.*

Day 35

*Every step I take in life
brings me closer to the Lord because
I am walking
to find my purpose and destiny.*

*As a person dedicated
to serving in the life of others
who do not know the way,
share God's love
through sharing and caring*

Day 36

*I never stop walking because
it drives me to do whatever I want to do.*

*Like going to work, dancing,
going out to eat, taking trips,
and going to the worship center
to praise God.*

*It allows me to share with others and
inspire them to do the same.*

Walking and never giving up.

Day 37

I take walks when I am
mad and need to let go of frustration.

If I hold that anger in,
it gives me headaches and heartache.

So, I walk to think about why I am angry.

And when I calm down
it allows me to let it go and
flow with a loving
spirit in life

Day 38

**What relaxes me is walking
through the park and
watching other people smile
when they walk by.**

Looking at the sun in the sky.

Singing a song as I walk along.

Thinking about what I did wrong.

And asking God to help make it right.

**It helps my life shine
while my day becomes better and brighter**

Day 39

The first time I started walking,
I was two years old.

I was sitting outside
playing with my brother.

My brother was on one side of the yard
and I was on the other side
watching him play.

Before I realized it,
I stood up and took a few steps.

Life is taking one step at a time.

Day 40

Walking has brought joy into my life because I have been to different places where there was laughter, love, and happiness.

Then for a minute, it went away. The silence made me feel lonely.

But the walk makes me laugh and love once again becoming happier for myself.

Day 41

Walking has brought the world to me via

traveling to many places. Trips that provides opportunities for meeting a lot of different people of different cultures.

**I have learned through life
that people are the same
no matter what color they are.**

Day 42

Walking this journey is long,
but I will not stop until
I cannot walk anymore.
Because to go somewhere
you have to start somewhere.

I am starting right now
in my community.

I believe that it will take me
to a place of change
mentally, emotionally,
physically, socially,
and spiritually.

Let's walk together
to make the difference.

Day 43

*Spring is here and
winter is leaving.*

*You can change into something
lighter and thinner, like jogging suits,
shorts, t-shirts, and pretty colors
that will brighten up your world.*

*Life is all about your world
and life is all about change.*

*Nothing stays the same
so let go of the winter weight
that keeps us warm and
shave off some pounds.*

*You can now put less on
to look good in the
springtime and summertime*

Day 44

*In your walk of life,
you have to believe in yourself.*

Keep trying until you get it right.

Everything takes time and patience.

*You have to find it in yourself
to be motivated.*

*Or have a strong support team
with motivation and dedication.*

*Once you become
motivated and determined,
nothing will stop your ambition.*

But remember it all starts in the mind.

*You will have to want it for yourself
because nobody can do it for you.*

Day 45

Laughter and joy will come

your way just when you let go of what is stopping you from laughing.

God never said we would not have bad days. However, the good thing is that the bad days will not last always.

You will never know how to let go if you never go through something in life.

There are many doors we will go through in life, but what

I have learned is how we come out is most important.

Keep walking and keep smiling because if you do you get another day to repent.

Day 46

Today was a quiet day.

But I walk in love
to offer someone a helping hand.

I walk with pain and hope
it does not remain the same.

Believing the Creator
is going to bring me through.

While I put a smile on somebody's face,
we never know
what we will face tomorrow.

But for today,
I feel good in the neighborhood
so I am going to keep
walking while I am breathing.

Day 47

Walking together with a friend
is nice because
you don't have to walk alone.

If you want to power walk,
walk by yourself.

You will do better
because it is hard
for someone else to keep up with
how fast you are walking.

You become more focused
on yourself and your goals.

You are more relaxed
and in tune with the universe.

But if you walk at a normal pace then,
you can walk together.

Day 48

You do not need anybody
to walk with
if you're walking with God.

You can talk to him,
see the things he created.

And hear the sounds of his creation.

It is beautiful to walk through all of it.
Because it changes
how you feel on a day
of amazing grace and love.

Day 49

*A great way to start your day
is an early morning walk.*

*It will get you in tune with
your mind, body, and soul.*

*It will work muscles
you have not worked in a while.*

*It will speak to your heart
and make you feel good
and remind you that you
are not walking alone.*

*You are walking
with the spirit of God
who created us and
taught us how to walk with*

Him

Day 50

**If your walk has caused
more sadness than happiness,
find another place to walk.**

There is always greatness somewhere.

Day 51

*When you feel stressed
walking is one of the best ways to let it go.*

*Because you can
talk it out with yourself,
think about it,
and find out how to get over it
by looking at different things.*

*Along the way,
you can take your mind off your stresses
and just appreciate your life
and how important it is to love you.*

Day 52

**Do not depend on the plan
you have for yourself.
God always has a better one.**

**Walk with God and
He will lead you down
the right path of life.**

**God knows what you need
and when He feels you are ready
God will bring it to your attention.**

Press on and keep walking.

Day 53

*Walking hand in hand
with someone you like
will make the heart grow stronger.*

*Every day will become something new
to learn about that someone.*

*How to lift each other
and have understanding.*

*The more you walk,
the more you will begin
to love each other the right way.*

*So, keep walking.
You never know if they are the right one.*

*Slow walks, open hearts, and a clear mind
will show you at the right time.*

Day 54

**There are many people I walk for
because they cannot walk for themselves.**

**That is greatness inspiring them
not to give up.**

**Their presence keeps hope alive
for their family and friends.
It also inspires me not to quit.**

**It is not all about the money.
But making a difference
in the lives of others
will make all the difference in ours.**

Day 55

There is no perfect time
to walk.

Just do it and
see how it makes you feel.

There is no special time to do it.

You can simply walk
at your own pace.

There is no rush.

If you want to start
with 5-minute walks.

Then start with that.
Do not let anybody
put pressure on you
to do more than you can.

In time you will be able
to pick up your pace.

Just keep walking and
before you know it
you will be walking more and more.

Day 56

*I walked out of my past
into my present,
and now into my future.*

*There is no reason
why I should look back.*

*Whatever happened in the past
has prepared me for right now.*

Do not look back and keep walking.

Day 57

*As I travel the roads
of this journey*

*I am amazed at all the great things
that have happened to me
and what I've made it through.*

Angels were watching out for me.

*And I'm grateful to the Creator
for allowing me to still be here.*

I will never stop walking with God.

He is worthy to be praised.

Day 58

As we walked,
we watched the sunset
and it's wonderful view.

To see the sun go down,
no man or woman can create
something so beautiful.

It lets us know
that someone greater than us
created that,
and it was God.

Day 59

When I walk on a cloudy day,
I can hear the thunder on the earth.

I can see the lightning in the sky.

You can feel the earth shake and tremble.

And then comes the rain-filled clouds
with the fullness of life in the sky.

I am reminded of the rain
and how it washes the earth clean
and feeds plants so they can grow.

Day 60

*Walking helps me to acknowledge
my strength and my health.*

*It gives me the confidence
to take care of myself
and to see my life clearer.*

*To understand what my body needs
--water, food, oxygen,
and a functioning nervous system.*

*We can last for a while
without food and water.
But our life would end immediately
without oxygen or
a working nervous system.*

*Let's keep on walking
and taking care of our bodies
for a life of health, happiness,*

and fulfillment

Day 61

*As I walk
through the storm of life,
I pray that it will end
and peace and happiness
will come together.*

*However, I stand on God's word
that He will never leave or forsake me
if I trust in him.*

So, keep walking and do not quit.

Do not give up.

*With God's love,
you will eventually
walk into his place of peace and happiness.*

Day 62

My life has changed so much by

walking. I feel like a new bride.

*Happy and content with everything, just
beautiful and being taken care of.*

*I can feel the light from up above
shining down on me.*

*The cool breeze
as I walk between the trees.*

*I hear the sound of leaves
making music as I talk to God
about my life and
how I am glad I'm in it.*

*I also talk about other things that I need.
Like God's love to keep me strong.*

*He helps to show how
to be in good health.
I am so grateful my prayers are heard,
and that He answers them.
God has advised me when
I do not have anyone to show me the way.*

Day 63

Every time I walk,
I get better and better
at reaching my goals.

It makes me want to get in shape,
eat right, and look good in my clothes.

I want to live a healthier life
so that I can be around to see my grand-
chrildren grow up and walk in their
dreams.

I want to see them sharing a life with the
ones they love.

I hope that they continue to keep walking
with me and live a healthy life.

Day 64

**They say
love conquers all.**

**If you love yourself,
you will do everything
in your power to do right by yourself.**

**Let's walk the right path
which is believing in you.
Anything you want or desire to do, go for
it!**

**Stop getting in your way.
Do not look at what others are doing.**

Look straight ahead and keep on walking!

Day 65

*There are times in our lives when
our hearts will be lonesome.*

*It will look for love to lift you up,
make you feel good,
or give you hope.*

*To move on from that lonely place,
love will find you when
you open your heart and
you will start doing for yourself again.*

*When I walk
sometimes my inner spirit
does not say anything.
It's just quiet for a while.*

*As time goes by,
I start smiling and
believing in myself again.
Thinking about things I want to do
and places I want to go.
All of that comes together
and love starts pouring out.*

*It will teach you to never wait for someone
to help you with your dreams or goals.*

Do it for yourself.

Day 66

I have walked
down the streets of sorrow
and learned that tomorrow
will be a better day.

If I shall wake up,
my life will start over again
with whatever that day brings.

You may have had
a thing on your list to do
but another thing
might be waiting for you.

Only God knows the real plans of your life.

Day 67

**Before we walked,
we crawled,
and then we started running.**

**It is amazing
how God created us as humans
to do all we can do.**

**Stand up and walk into your destiny.
And live your best life.**

**Whatever happens from there
keep doing you
and do not look back.**

Day 68

Walking
is something almost
anyone can do.

Whether it is walking in the park,
to the store, to school,
or even to a friend's house,
walking is a way of life
that enables you to get around.

It is nice to have friends to walk with
and talk to until you separate.

They become like clouds in the sky.

Friends come and go.
They rain like teardrops
that fall from your eyes
and you never know
when they will leave your life.

Enjoy each moment that you share
because every part of it will teach
you something about yourself.

Day 69

*I had a teacher who liked to
walk around the graveyard
instead of a park.
It's quiet and relaxing there.*

*I never walk around the graveyard but,
I know it is peaceful
because everybody is sleeping
and I visit it from time to time.*

*You do not have to worry
about anybody following you
because they are all dead.*

Day 70

**While we will walk
down different streets in life,
you will see they are all alike.**

**People live there and they seem
to be doing the same thing
year after year.**

**Nothing is going to change
until you move on,
walk in a different place
and decide to go in a different direction.**

Life is about what you make of it.

Day 71

*I learned in life that sometimes
you think you are walking
with somebody and the whole time
you were walking by yourself.*

*I found out that the person
I was walking with
was not on the same path
and we were different.*

*It was more about what they wanted
than what we both needed.*

*They had more negative energy
than positive energy
which caused us
to be walking together but alone.*

*Be careful who you choose
for your walking partner
and choose yourself first.*

Day 72

Every time I walk,
I get stronger and stronger.
I am better in the way I think,
the way I eat,
the people I am around,
and in my relationship with God.

The troubling times in my life
are not gone
but they are easier to deal with.

The struggle is real
but I have learned
it is just a part of life
so I walk with it and handle
life's challenges much better.

Day 73

**Walking
has built up my
self-esteem and it makes me smile.**

**I feel better when
I look at myself in the mirror.**

**When I see the extra weight
I have gained I do not feel bad
because I am walking to lose it all.**

**In looking at myself
I have gained the confidence
to like myself
with or without the extra weight
because I walk to keep it down.**

Day 74

**When you start walking
try little steps until
you are ready to take more**

.

**Five-minute walks are good.
And when you feel like walking 10 minutes,
then do it but do not quit.**

**Keep going until you get up to 30 minutes
or to even an hour.**

**Then you can look back
at your progress
and talk about how you did it.**

Day 75

Stop weeping and start walking.
Nothing is going to work
until you make a move.

The longer you sit around
and complain about it
the longer it is going
to take you to get started.

I remember I used to weep
about getting out there and walking.

I would walk with friends,
co-workers, and family.

When they stopped walking,
then I would stop.

Until one day I just started
walking and talking and
I was still going by myself.

Day 76

**When I started walking
in my neighborhood
I didn't know
people were watching me
throughout the complex.**

**Until one day a man said to me,
"I didn't see you walking today".**

**And said,
how he "needs to get back
out there and walk".**

**The next day I saw him walking.
It made me feel good
to inspire someone
to get back on track and walk.**

Day 77

*Walking
has become my passion.*

*It helps me to stay focused
and keeps me on track.*

*Whenever I feel like
I have gained too much weight,
I start walking and working out.*

*I fall short sometimes
because I love food but,
I am beginning to love myself more.*

*So, I'm going to push harder
to eat right while I walk
and inspire others to do the same.*

Day 78

**Walking
is good for everybody
no matter how big, small, short, tall,
young, or old.**

**We all need to walk
to live a healthy life,
strengthen our bones
and improve our balance in life.**

Day 79

**When you walk in the park,
you will love God's creation.**

The sky, the earth, the water, and the sun.

**Walking
will make you feel good
as well as look good.**

**And when you get home,
you will be able to relax and say my walk**

was beautiful.

Day 80

When I am feeling down,
I like going for a walk.
It helps me to feel better.

It gives me time to think things over,
cry them out, and laugh.

Walking reminds me that
nothing lasts forever and
everything comes to an end.

Day 81

**Some people walk
in the rain just to hear
the different sounds it makes
on the pavement.**

**Some people like walking
in the rain with the one they love.**

**I like walking in the rain
just so I can see it fall from the sky.**

**It is so amazing to see
how great God is to this world.**

Day 82

I started walking down the street
and ended up on the other side of town.

And saw some of my friends
so we all started walking.

It is a good feeling
when you have someone to walk with
because we get to talk and laugh together.

Before you know it t
he day is done and ready to end.

Day 83

I only went for a walk
to be alone for a little while.

Everybody needs to get away
from the crowd because
the crowd and noise
can get loud sometimes.

And you need peace of mind.

Walking is one of the best ways
to be alone and find peace.

Day 84

Walking
brings out the best in me.

It allows my mind to run free.

It releases everything
that is on the inside
and allows me to let go
of negative thoughts and feelings.

As well as dream about what I want.

Day 85

*We are going to walk
up to a lot of doors
before we get to the right one
we want to go through.*

*If you want something in life
there is nothing too hard for you.*

Day 86

**When you walk more
you are less stressed
because you use that energy exercising.**

Let go of your stress into the air.

**And breathe in something new
to start your day.**

Day 87

*I can not walk as fast
but I still walk in my old age.*

*I can't run
but I make every step count.*

*Walking has kept me going
for as long as I lived.*

Day 88

Any place you walk
is good as long as you walk.

If you walk on the job,
you are walking.

If you walk in the store,
you're walking.

If you walk in the park---
you are walking!

And if you do not walk too far
that is still walking.

It does not matter as long as you walk.

Day 89

Life is too short

not to walk into your dreams.

Because if you do not take the first step, you

will never see those dreams come

true.

Day 90

If you do not walk through it,
you never know what
is waiting on the other side of the door.

Take a chance
and you will learn something
one way or another.

It will help you to know

Day 91

**Walk as if it were
your last days on the earth.**

Enjoy your life as time passes by.

**You never know
what will happen the next day.**

Day 93

*I will always love
to walk no matter what.*

*Walking has been my peace i
n a time of stress.*

*It comforted me
when I had no one to talk to.*

*It makes me strong when
I feel tired and even helps me sleep.*

Day 94

*Walking has treated
me like a best friend.*

*Always there for me.
Always listening when I talk.*

*It lets me cry
and does not tell me not to.*

*It lets me shine
just like the sun above.*

*It lets me say
what's on my mind
all the time.*

And that is why I love to walk.

Day 95

**I think nothing of walking fast
until I met someone who walks slowly.**

**So, I have learned to slow down when
I walk with different people.**

**Everybody is not going
to walk the same way.**

Day 96

*A thirty-minute walk
will change how we feel.*

*It will help you to lose weight
and feel great.*

*If you are in a bad mood
or have been arguing,
your walk will help you
think better about what
you just went through.*

Walking is good for you.

Day 97

Walk out of that negative life
into a positive one.

And start hanging out with people
who want the same thing you want.

Pursue love and happiness!

Day 98

Walk with the ones
who walk with you.

Walk away from people
who do not want anything out of life.

They will do nothing
but hold you down.

Day 99

**Be careful who
you let walk in your life.**

**Someone can do more harm
than help you if they
do not have anything to bring to the table.**

**Even while disappointing,
let them walk.**

Day 100

*I was walking down
the road called "love"
and found I was on the wrong street.*

It was jealousy.

*You see low self-esteem,
poor self-image, and bad values.*

*There was nothing confident
about this road.*

*It was hard to get by
because it was an unbelievable place.*

I told myself, "this can't be love."

*When I looked up and put on my glasses,
the street sign read
"jealousy" instead of "love."*

Day 101

*I love to hear the sound
of my feet patting on the ground.*

*When I walk it's a
blessing to me and
anyone else who is watching.*

There is always somebody to inspire.

About the Author

My name is Lawanda Armstrong- Jackson. I am a native of New Jersey, relocated to Florida with a dream to make a difference with people from all walks of life. In the process of it all, make a difference in my life.

I have learned that my purpose here on earth is to do God's will before my home going. I realize that if I let go of my past and everything that I held inside, I could move forward with my father's plan. So I say to you, let go and let God direct your life.